REAL ME

There always comes a point in life while living alone and fighting for existence when our instinct turns back asking the toughest question humanity have never understood; for what I'm facing all this pain and sorrow? Why only me?

I cannot describe those tough thirty minutes when for a while tough thoughts absorb me into their own world of dominating questions every day making my body still with prevailing dying man like feeling inside as if a soldier is looking back toward his lost battle.

I think I'm lost somewhere in time and here every direction I look into seems like a new beginning. It's a bizarre of dreams and imaginations I am trapped in. Every direction I go brings me at the same point I started from, it forms a never-ending loop of confusion and death trap. I'm not learning from life but losing it.

I ask myself if I am dying?

This is less a question, more a painful paradox. Death and life are not the terms understood well.

It happens so often when even we are dying, we cannot die completely and neither life allows us to live.

Life says "I will give you that enough in which you can survive but not enough to grow". This is where it traps a person in its never-ending drama, escaping from there counts sacrifices we cannot afford.

We cannot veil the importance of this moment with layers of pain and frustration because it's a feeling that bores out your individual reality. It brings us on verge of enlightenment. It frees us from all joy, fear, expectations and shows us practical things.

Unlike happiness, that is superficial and teaches nothing, frustration is a deep thing that unveils 'real you'.

I started exploring things, gathering information bit by bit as if getting an answer have become more important than running for food and shelter. If I am dying, I don't want to waste my remaining life messing with the same death trap.

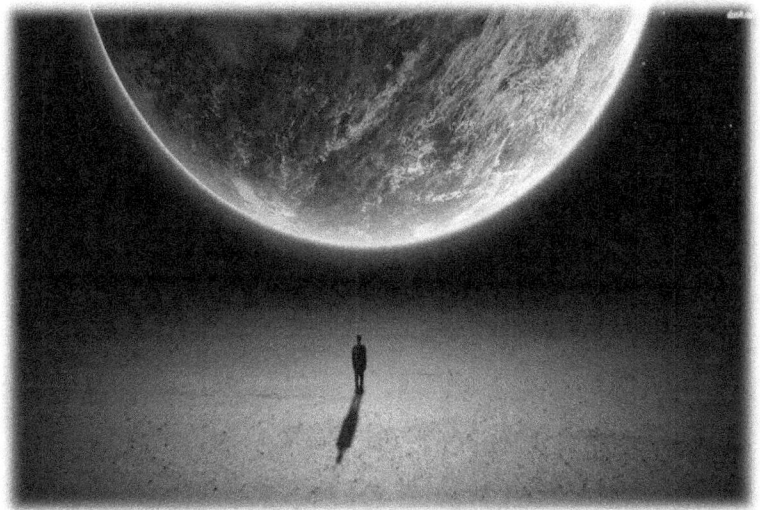

The way we cannot feel the earth round until we observe from space. There must be some cause that our eyes cannot see, organs cannot sense, brain cannot understand until we free ourselves from limitations and observe events from distance. I am searching that higher vision.

The way for a man flying on an airplane; tiny grasses and giant trees seem equal and dissolved to form a giant landmass, whose extent he can define from there. For a person with higher perspective, world dissolves into the same state.

Once we start rising, subjects seem to become worthless. Everyone becomes equal before the eyes, definition of high and low vanishes, terms like up and down 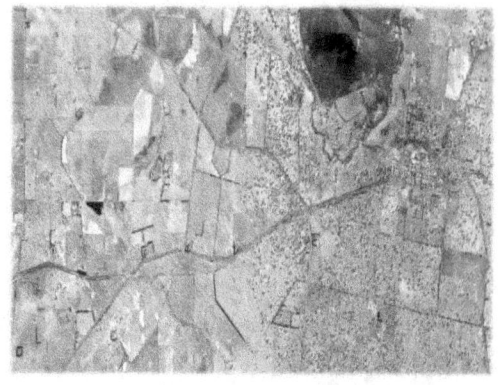 becomes meaningless. It needs a hard push to jump that higher.

All I have understood about the way life works is here we all are creating impressions in our minds from the things we experience every day. We manipulate it through logic and intelligence and by doing so we define our own picture of reality that is never universal but just a mere individual illusion.

These illusions can interact and influence the portions of individual realities with communication and experiences and so form an everlasting trap of society.

This is not me who can feel things, who knows you and others, who do things for some cause; but it's the illusion that has trapped me.

Everyone in this world have their own aspect of reality that in simple word we call perspective. Individual perspective defines the fate.

Fate is a collapsed state of superposed reality.

In this world, things exist in multiple possible states at the same time. They acquire one single value only when we observe them.

Perspective is an interpretation of this collapsed superposed reality. We can either chose to define perspective as per observation or define it first and then observe things.

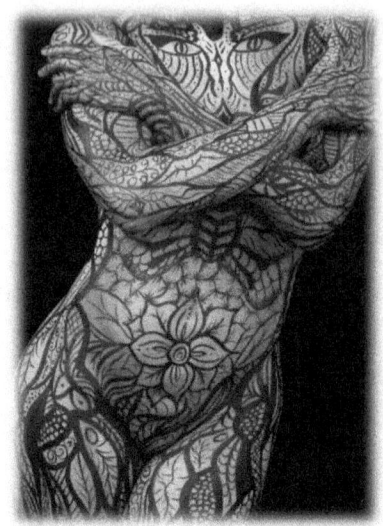

 In both the cases, the result will be the same.

 We mostly have pre-defined perspective. The good and bad results we see in life are culmination of them.

Perspective of looking at something defines the manner we are going to channel our energy towards it and this energy defines the fate of that entity. It's a subconscious process, nothing happens superficially.

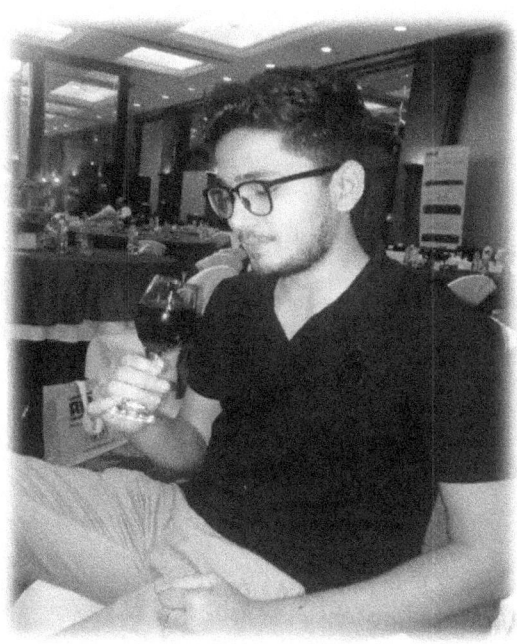

For example; if we are holding a glass of red wine in hand and our perspective of looking things around is of love, we leave it unharmed. It happens because we channelize our energy in keeping things nice and subtle.

Our thought has manipulated our will here to preserve things.

In the same manner, if our perspective of looking at things around is of hate, our subconscious mind channelizes energy towards destructive goal that may result in smashing the glass against the floor or wall.

Here our thought has manipulated our will to destroy things.

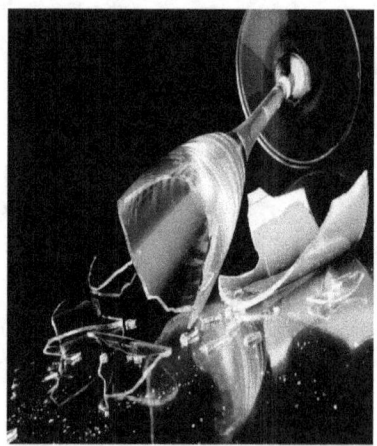

The example above describes active result of manipulation of reality through thoughts in which they directly influence the object through the body to define their fate.

There is a never ending passive result of the same. By leaving the signs of hate and negativity in the room we smashed the glass transfers the same message into the environment and gets added as a new page into your book of reality that is ugly and negative.

The thought itself and the perspective of looking at the result followed by it is called reality. A sequence of such realities defines who the person is and where his fate will take him?

Sir Adolf Hitler was an insignificant person until he thought he was insignificant.

Becoming a dictator could have never become a part of his reality until he started speaking in mass, expressing his thoughts and began dreaming of controlling it.

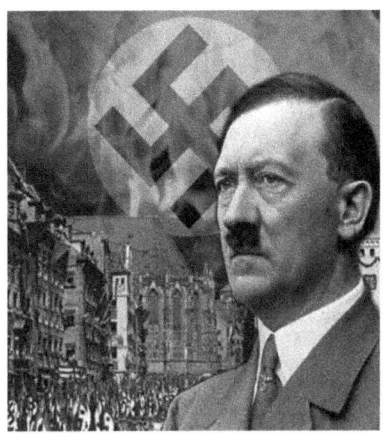

If it had never happened, he could also be one among the 20 million dead people during the First World War. His thoughts, dreams and vision were collectively pointing towards a new reality that had existence only in thoughts and then became real.

This was the passive result of his perspective of looking at things and himself.

Watching people dying around, you better know the pain of losing loved ones, creates irresistible frustration.

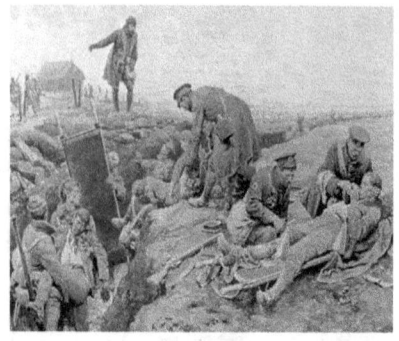

The time when Germany was starving, there was no hope that anyone can grow from the ground out of this frustration.

Germany could have grown rich and elite Hitler. Becoming such a large dictator, medals and awards for bravery and promotion in army is not enough.

But believe, these awards generated the feeling of being superior in his mind. Here award is just an object but the perspective of looking at it gave him the feeling of pride and feeling of being superior. It already transformed him to become a braver person and a leader. This was the point where his fate started taking shape.

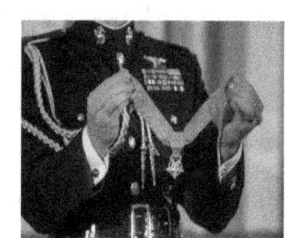

When the entire nation was brimming with negativity, he was flourished with positive thought that definitely made him a better race and he conquered.

Fate is all about the way we see and judge things around. If we see negative, our fate goes against us. If we see positive, our fate goes with us. This is how god has programmed our strings.

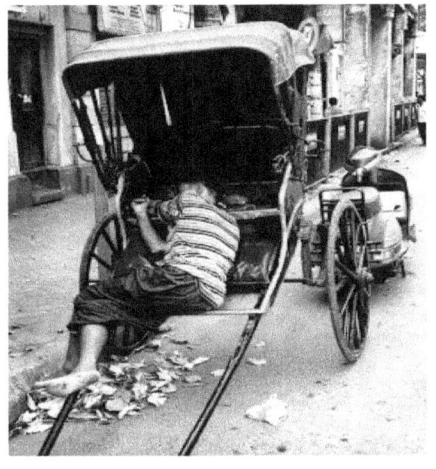

The fate of a normal Rikshaw puller is two times meal daily because his brain doesn't allow him to think beyond that level. The subconscious mind starts working here and channelizes the energy in the way to make two times meal for him available daily.

The reality he creates for himself contains dreams, past life records, people he meets and everything else is confined within his fate.

In similar way, the fragment of reality defined by an entrepreneur or a potential entrepreneur growing in some poor region of uneducated mass could have formed same like the Rikshaw puller's one. Since reality is just an individual creation, instead of being same, the world defined by him varies and seems more opportunistic.

There is a beautiful scientific illustration of this fact above.

A thought experiment was once performed by Nobel Prize winning physicist Sir Erwin Schrödinger that cemented his status in world of physics.

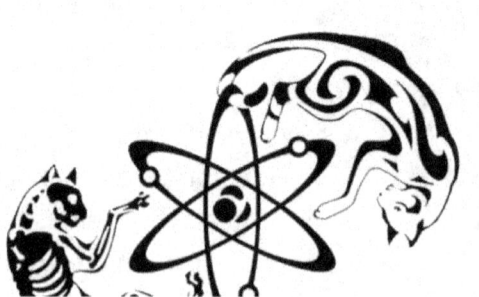

The experiment is famous as Schrödinger 's Cat Paradox.

In his thought experiment, he places a cat in a steel box along with a Geiger counter, a hammer, radioactive substance and a vial of poison.

If the Geiger counter detects decay of the radioactive substance it triggers the hammer and poison gets released which subsequently kills the cat.

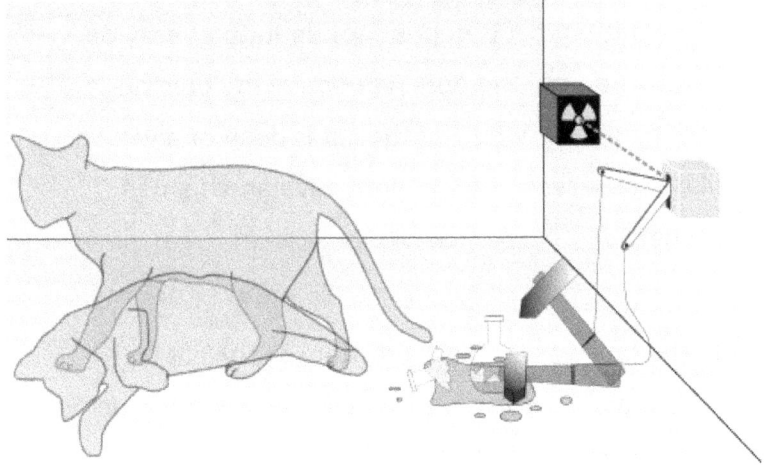

Decay of a radioactive substance happens randomly, and we cannot predict the time when it is going to happen because atoms exist both decayed and not decayed at the same time in a state called superposition.

When the radioactive substance decays, the Geiger detects it and triggers the hammer to release the poison, which subsequently kills the cat.

Here the fate of cat is dependent upon the decay of the atom. So until the observer opens the box, he cannot figure out whether the cat is dead or alive. So until it is observed, it stays both alive and dead in equal parts.

Until the box was opened, the state of the cat is unknown and therefore, the cat is considered to be both alive and dead at the same time until it is observed.

"If you isolate the cat, you have to treat it as if it is doing all of the possible things—being alive and dead—at the same time.

If you try making predictions and you assume you are knowing the status of the cat, you could be wrong.

You will be right if you assume that it's in combination of all possible states.

Immediately upon looking at the cat, the observer knows the state and superposition collapses to attain one single state.

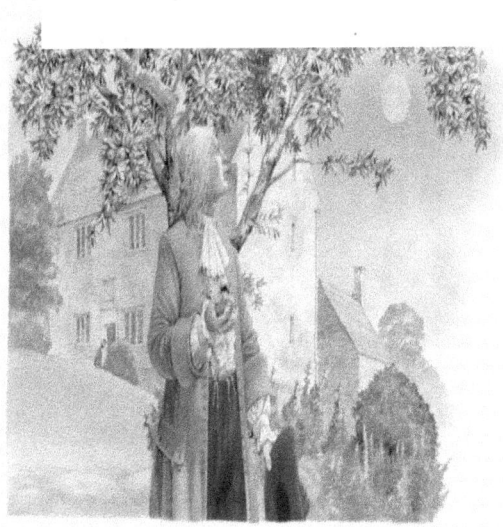

We can also say, there was no gravity before Newton discovered it. Humans had never experienced a force pulling them down until gravity was discovered.

Now we all feel like being on an ocean bed of something pushing us down. I am not talking about the restrictions of flying without wings.

We never cared if there was a such force even before it's discovery.

Now since we have observed it, the superposition of gravity has collapsed down to one state that says gravity exists.

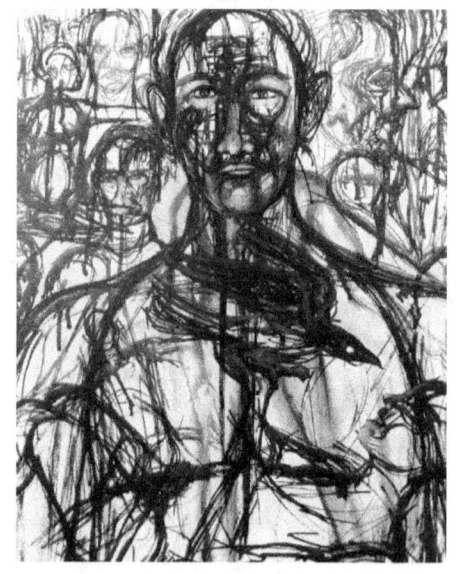

We have got the answer to our very first question with which the chapter started; 'for what I'm facing all this pain and sorrow? Why only me?'

Only me, because I am the only person responsible for my fate. My present condition, my emotional state, those painful thoughts are reflections of the reality that I have defined by myself.

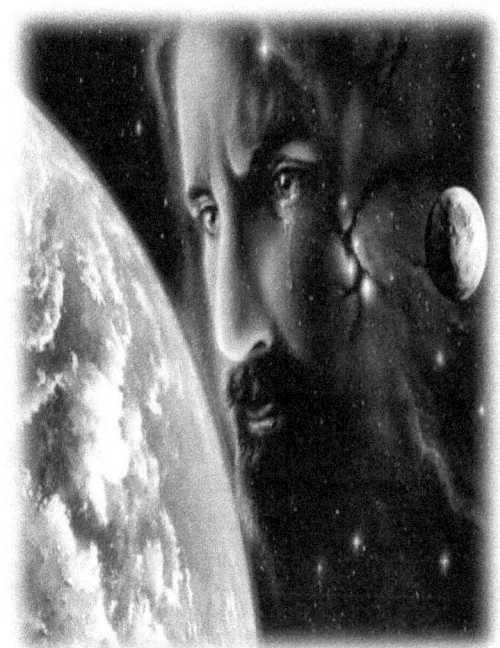

The fragments of impression of experiences stored in my mind as knowledge had an initial negative perspective while being stored by virtue of which my fate got defined.

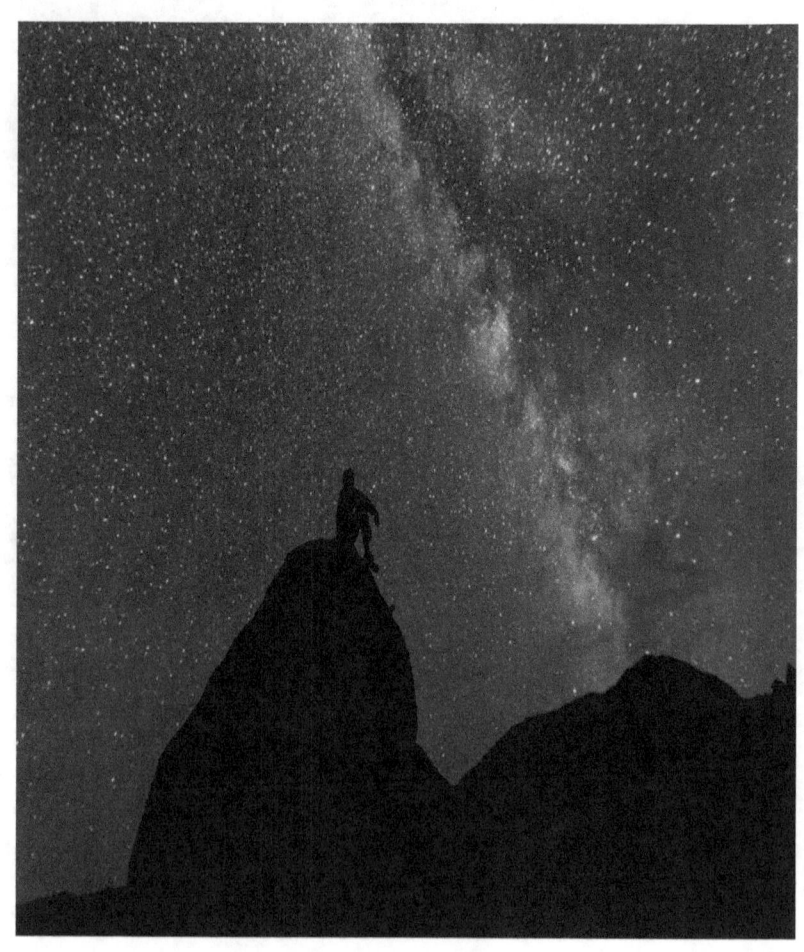

The Illusion of Existence

Is this entire Universe alive? Is there any God?
Have you ever questioned the reason of your existence? Have you ever thought about the goal of your life?

Doesn't questions like this sometimes becomes un-tolerable that even after pondering for hours we hit with no solution and term it "God's creation".

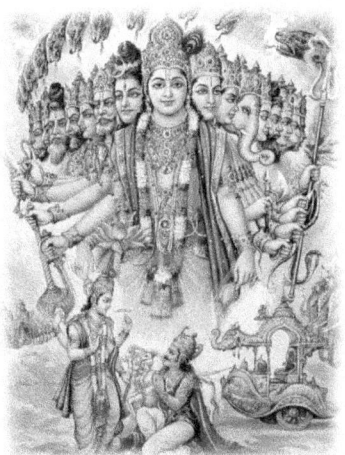

We have been worshipping God since ages yet we have no idea about his identity, we don't even have any proof of his existence and have no idea about his form.

In this chapter we are going to understand one such complex invention of Universe or God's creation – Life.

Understanding the concept of life is an essential key to understand the concept of God.
Further we are going to use the same discussion to qualify the existence of god.

Although motion is a sign of life but this property only is not sufficient to generalize our understanding for life on the cosmic scale.

On earth, qualifying life on the basis of motion and reproductive ability sounds perfect but if we alter our perspective of looking at life from earth to the reference of cosmos then everything we see is continuously moving with respect to some reference and we find nothing at absolute rest as Einstein also says in his theory of Special Relativity.

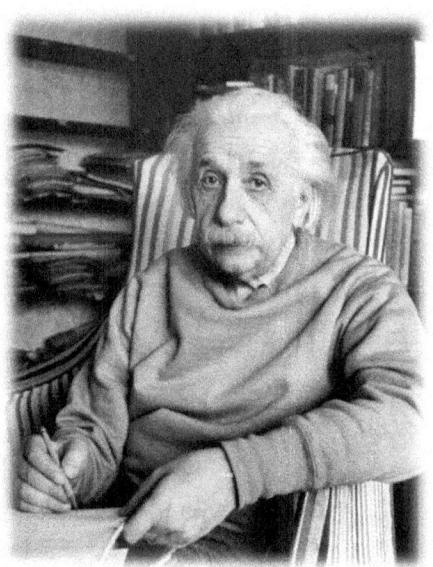

Can we say then, all these moving objects are alive?

Before we answer to this question we need to take a look from different perspective. If we try to qualify life from its ability to reproduce, only then we get a hit that they can't reproduce and so they are not alive.

Darwin writes in his famous theory of evolution that in course of evolution there are two ways a race can choose for survival.

If the conditions are favorable to life, cells choose to reproduce and pass on their own being and if adverse then instead of choosing to reproduce, they choose to make themselves live longer that is the path of immortality.

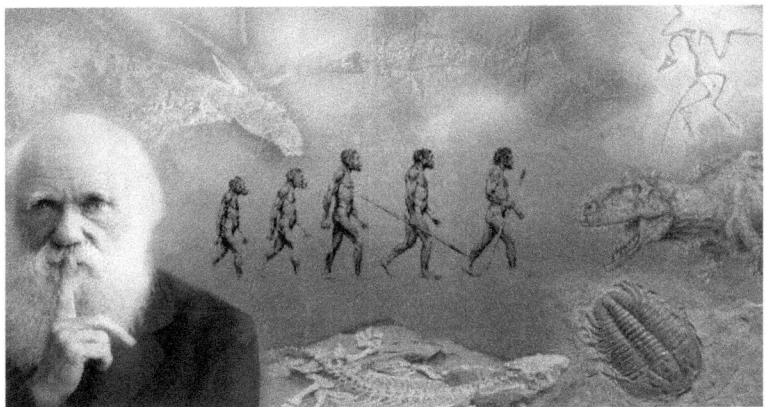

So these are two basic concepts through which we qualify life and clearly these are neither completely applicable on earth nor from the reference of Universe.

On one hand where on earth, things that can move can either reproduce or cannot reproduce to follow immortality.

Same on the cosmic scale, there happens two things, the things that can move; like planets and stars, either remain immortal or gets recreated in places like nebulae and gas clouds.

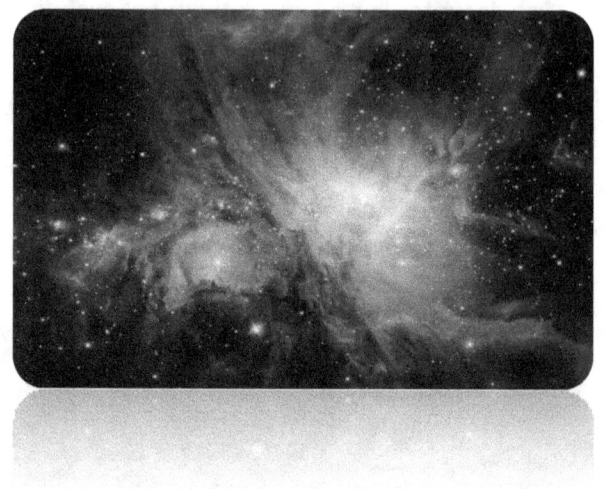

This scenario is quite similar to the scenario of life on earth and is creating confusion with qualifying life.

Life is mainly seen with its chemical and physical complexity of hundreds of processes at a time. For having a generalized definition of life, every single process must fit with the definition.

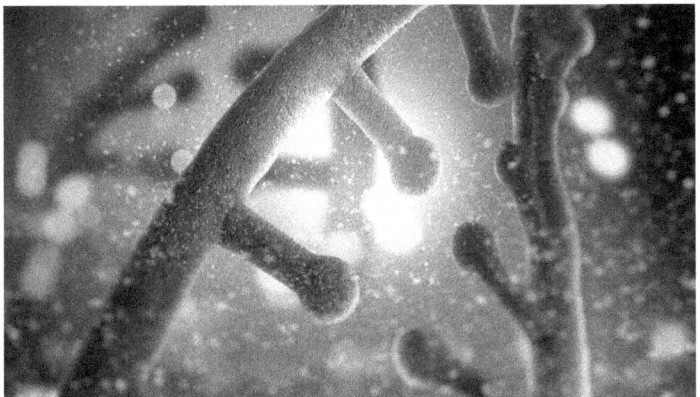

Here the major factors that qualifies life does not satisfy our intuition of qualifying it. The planets and stars that our intuition states non-living shows life like property from definition.

For a deeper understanding we will further drill to the molecular level and see if there is some secret hidden in carbon hydrogen relationship.

Before we proceed further, let's assume anything that has ability to harmonize changes within itself through its own functionalities is alive. I think this assumption fits on a generalized scale.

In this universe almost everything existing bears this incredible property. Everything in this universe is stable and does not want changes. You can take a planet, a stone on the seashore, the homogeneity of atmospheric air and water in ocean.

Everything likes to be balanced. Throw a ball from height, it will keep moving until all forces on it are balanced. Leave a cup of hot coffee on the table, it will radiate until it attains the temperature of room.

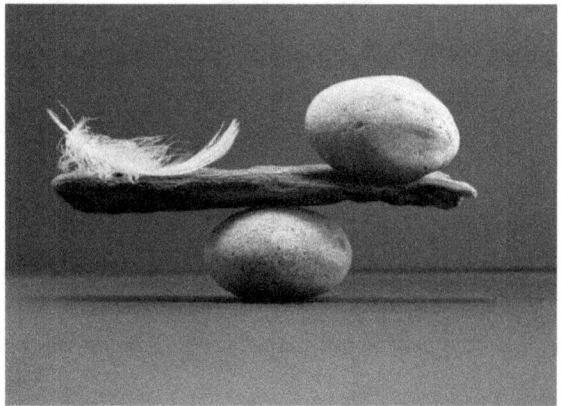

The rotation of electrons around the positively charged nucleus give rise to the atoms whose various clusters or groups gives rise to the molecules. Which further forms various substances having various properties.

It keeps maintaining the balance. Sometimes these substances form network to maintain their balance through various small processes.

Sometimes these processes get complex that an automated cycle of various different processes gets initiated within the same network, in which one process disturbs the balance of other and other processes gets initiated to balance it.

Life is also an automated cycle of dis balancing and balancing processes within an entity.

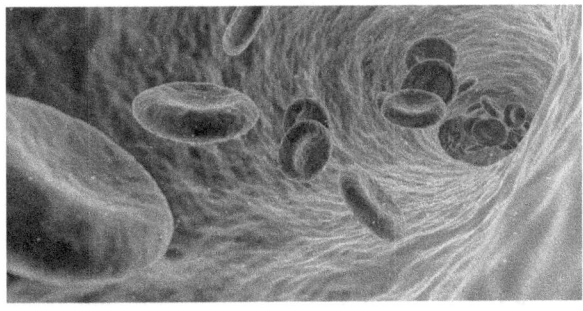 When formation of network of these processes goes on and on, a time comes when it gets so complex so that we can picture a complete different machine engaged in its own activities as a result. This is the stage of formation of living cells from where we can distinguish all dis balancing processes as a whole different process and all balancing processes on higher scale as a different process.

The terms like hunger, food affinity etc. are the outcomes of the same network of dis balancing processes and the terms like eating, drinking, growing, excreting etc. are the outcomes of the network of balancing processes.

On earth, the network of carbon and hydrogen have won the race and has become the basis of all existing life forms.

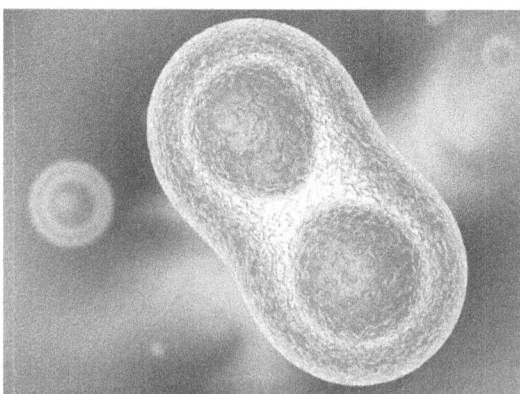

The processes within such networks are just basic chemistry and physics but because of complexity biology deals them on a larger scale.

Apart from Carbon and Hydrogen, other elements too could have formed life but because of its property of forming wide range of possible compounds on earth has made these two elements win the race.

Here every defined process in a network is giving rise to some higher. Our lifestyle is also defined so can we also be a part of something grand?

For an instance if the basic building blocks of body, the cells, get intellect then even if they somehow establish the fact that their life in vicinity of each other is giving rise to something high, a tissue, still they can never deduce the fact that these tissues are also alive.

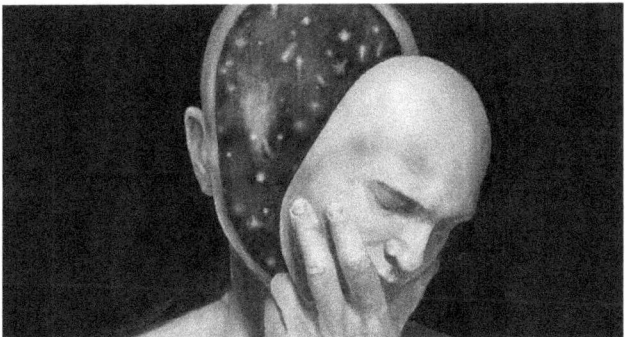

Their perspective of looking at living world would only be confined to the fact that they are the only alive beings and they are living their own life, in their own way. They are consuming food, protecting their lives, reproducing and growing.

But while doing so the food and activity chain network they form gets complex in such manner that the network too starts living its own life in its own way – simple dis balancing and balancing of processes. The next network so formed by such networks are also living their own lives in their own ways.

Vicinity of Individual living organisms like cells have given rise to an entirely different life form of cellular clusters whose further network gets so complex on a large scale that they give rise to a living body like of a Human being.

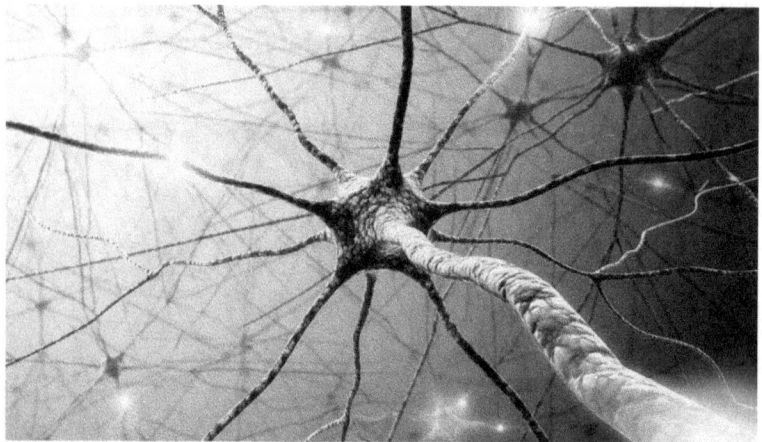

Every life form at every stage hardly knows the fact that their existence is dependent on some other life form. And even if they know it, they can never feel it. As we humans know it very well that individual living cells are our building blocks still we can't feel them as separate organisms and we perceive them as our own part.

If we think a bit deeply we can have a feel of it. So what is a living body? It's just a complex network of various physical and chemical processes formed by non- living particles giving rise to basic life forms embedded on a non-living base or floating in a non-living medium in a network. Say humans, made of dead and living cells, with some floating in a medium of water and other substances, namely blood, forming a very complex network running various processes.

So, if it is all about complexity of processes and cannot have a generalized definition on that basis, then we can say either everything is alive or life is just an illusion.

Life is a paradox and it cannot be defined and talking about it is completely inconsistent. It might seem difficult to except this fact because our intuition to life has developed in the course of thousands of years, but it is true.

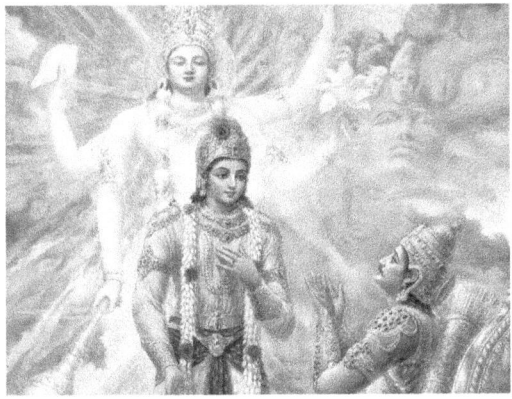

Life is an illusion have made many facts of ancient Hindu Vedic epic Bhaagwad Gita clear in a single go.

So, from the discussion above, it's clear there's no such big illusion than the life itself.

Now let us come back to our initial discussion. Is God alive? No, if there is any God, we cannot qualify his state with a parameter which is itself an illusion.

DIMENSIONS

Our perception is very confined to the world we see. Our dreams, desires, thinking ability and everything else remains very limited.

This world is not that limited, it's much broader that we cannot even perceive. Bhagwat Gita, the book that I believe to be more scientific than religious also talks about something similar.

There is a huge matrix of dimensional complexity where new dimensions appear and go.

It is said for the person who attains the ultimate state of intellect or even gets closer to the divine being, all illusions (Maya) of relationship and worldly feelings vanishes. This statement stands on a very strong scientific and mathematical foundation.

Also, in Shreemad Bhagwat Gita when Lord Krishna says to Arjun that through his normal eyes he cannot see his entire being as he was so huge and extended into all directions, there was a use of strong scientific base for describing God in this way.

There is a very complex interplay of dimensions that makes the world so interesting.

Before drilling deeper, let's start with understanding the meaning of dimension.

For an event to be defined in a frame of reference, the minimum number of coordinates needed is the order of dimension for that frame.

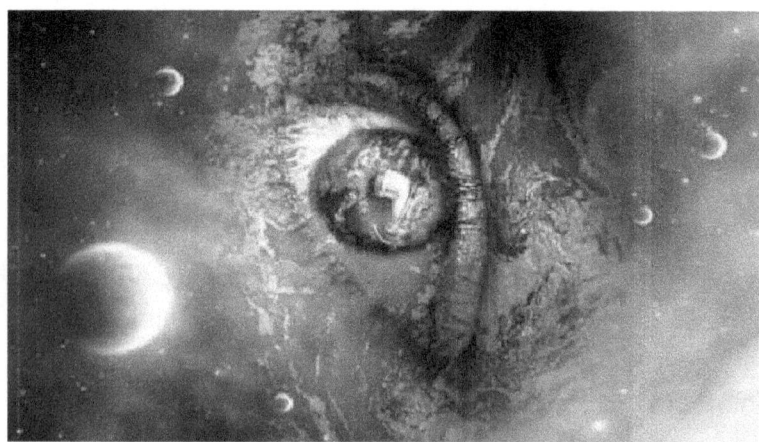

Here by an event, it doesn't mean an occurrence, event can be anything existing either in real or into the imagination.

So, for a point to be defined in its own frame, the minimum number of coordinates needed is zero. That means a point is a zero-dimensional figure.

Dimensions don't remain confined to themselves, they can regenerate or dissolve.

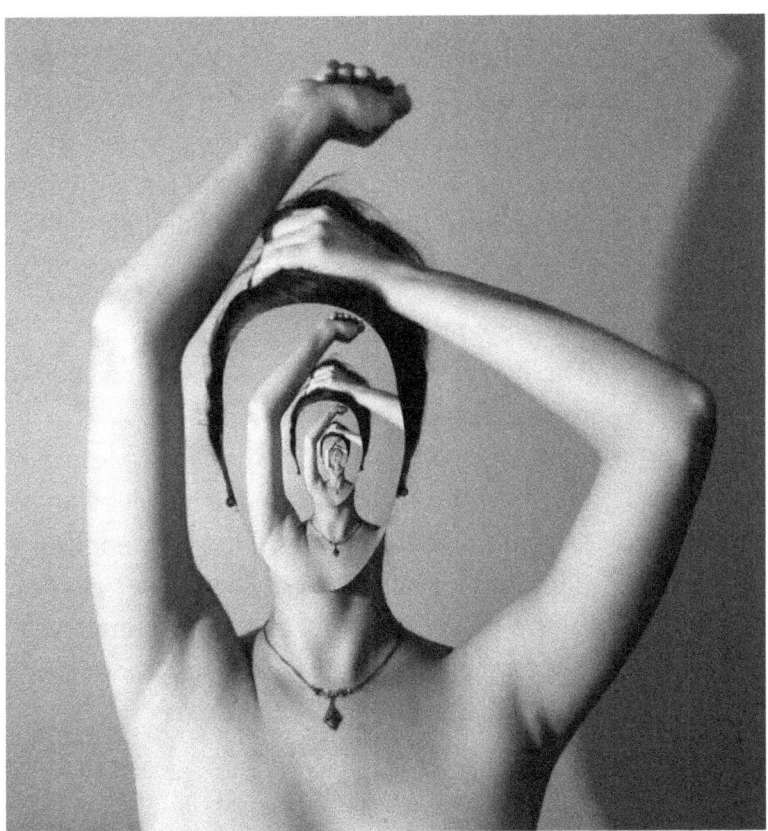

Take an ant for example. It cannot even see the person laying footprints on the ground. It can only see the result because the significant height scale for an ant lies in our negligible frame in day to day observation. For it, the footprint would have appeared all of a sudden. The section of foot that the ant could see was a segment of negligible height of our giant body. The segment seen by the ant dissolves into just two dimensions in the perspective of human observer. Until lifted to a significant height, the ant cannot even imagine the giant laying it or until that dissolved dimension is resolved.

Assuming it to be a two-dimensional organism, living in forms of straight lines on a piece of paper. There will be no way it can enter into a circle drawn on the same plane. Being a three-dimensional organism, if human draws even a dot inside that circle, for an ant observing it, will be an unpredictable event. It would be something happened all of a sudden. Here for us, drawing a dot could be as easy as putting and lifting a pen but here for the ant confined to that plane, there exists nothing like height so it cannot define the cause of that event.

There are infinite ways of drawing a dot into that circle but for an organism confined to two dimensions only, there is no such way.

You can imagine every single way of drawing a dot into it as a line piercing through the plane; there you will find infinite such lines passing through it.

This means, for a region of lower order dimension existing in a dimension of higher order, there exists infinite ways of manipulating an event inside it by accessing the dimension of higher order.

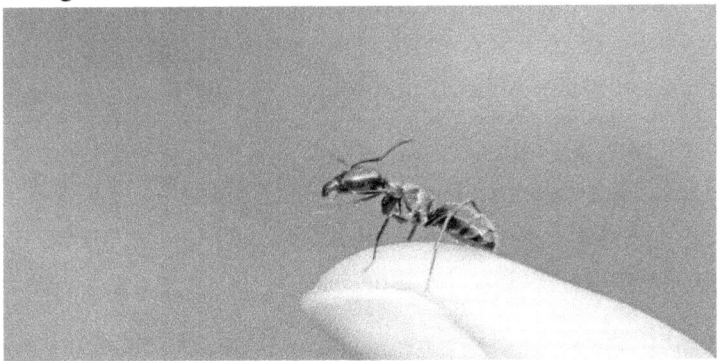

Multiple order dimensions co-exist, they get revealed only when certain event happens through them.

If we lift the ant from the paper, we can keep it anywhere inside that circle.

Same applies to the perception of the ant while defining the appearance of foot prints on the ground.

We have to provide an additional vision to the ant by introducing the height component. If we pick it to certain height, then only it can or whole being.

If we take this concept to the religious perspective, as mentioned in Shri Mad Bagwatam, we find Lord Krishna provided *divya drishti* or a superior vision to Arjuna to see his grand being.

Dimensional regeneration is not only limited to the world we call real or its not limited to the mathematical grounds of solid geometry only but it applies everywhere.

We can take example of space-time. Here time is a dimension of infinite intersections with space and so happens events and we find things moving through time frame even if they are standing still.

Sometimes I try to place myself away from all worldly pursuits. I observe this body both alive and dead at the same time, the same way we can see a society from sky while we cannot see even a single complete house from a room.

This human life is very limited and tough to understand, everything seems preplanned. We are designed in a way to think we are going to last forever. We are made to think always that future is better.

www.ingramcontent.com/pod-product-compliance
Lightning Source LLC
Chambersburg PA
CBHW070318240526
45467CB00046B/2032